Behind the Smile

Written By: Sleight

Edited By:
Chelsea Timmons
Robert E. Timmons II
ShaLayla J. Simmons

Illustration By:
Jai Haley

Photography By:
Anita Porché-Garcia

ISBN: 978-1-5356-1353-8

Acknowledgements

To those that inspire me,
The one that loves me,
The one that has sacrificed for me,
The one that supports me, and
The one that pushes me to my best
Thank you.

Contents

BEHIND THE SMILE

Prelude

You never know what's going on in someone's life until you look behind their smile...

BEHIND MY SMILE

Behind my smile you will travel on the winding roads of my doubts
which have always delayed, but never stopped my progress.
You will climb the immense mountain ranges of my adversity,
and marvel at the scenic views they create,
or you will turn away, and try to walk around the challenge—
because to be honest, I've done both.

You will sail on the vast oceans of my heart,
passing the rolling hills of red violets and
endless valleys of blue roses
as you feel the gentle push and pull of my love,
but you'll also experience the storms of my heartbreak,
and be hit by the quiet, yet fierce breeze of my lust.

Behind my smile you will soar on the
wings of my faith
and feel the
embrace
of my freedom.
But if you look closely you'll see...I'm missing some feathers.
And I have some unhealed scars.
And one of my wings is broken.
You will witness my struggle
to maintain my altitude, and
with my faith and his strength, I will.
Prayerfully.

When you look behind my smile you will
discover the complexities of my story and
take a journey through my life,
and maybe, you'll be able to understand

Me.

T.E.A.R.S

When I cry, you won't see tears fall from my eyes;
it's not that my sorrow doesn't exists,
it's just merely wearing a disguise.
See, when I cry my pace is a little slower,
my words are a little colder, and my body is a
little numb…

When I cry my feet no longer have a set course;
they walk in circle, after circle, after circle,
forming a circumference that's cheerless.
It's six-foot radius keeps me bound to my
anguish,
three hundred and sixty degrees of blues,
never ending…

When I cry, I see the worst in things around me;
I no longer see the blooming of flowers,
but I see the withering away of their petals.
I don't see birds gracing the sky in glorious flight;
I see vultures circling their prey.
My hope is demolished—
all that's left is pain and strife getting in the way,
and I can see my happiest moments
turning gray…

When I cry, my whole body reacts;
if you look closely, you can see the collapsing of
my back,
my fist clinched tight.
The cringing in my body
and the - s t r a i n - in my muscles,

and my hands longing to wipe away these non-
existing tears from my face.
The quivering of my lips,
and the sniffling of my nose.
With each movement I make, my pain overtakes
my body and I am consumed.

I confine myself to my room, so this infection
doesn't spread.
I fall to my knees with my hands on my head—
I bang my fist on the ground, making an earth
quake with each pound.
I throw my head back and I look up to heaven.

There's a rumbling in my gut.
No, deeper—
there's a rumbling in my soul.
It starts rising as my emotions take control.
There's a piercing sound quick like lightening,
orchestrated from my soul but then released from
my throat,
"HELP ME, GOD!"

I fall, and I lie flat on my back.
The only sound is the beat of my heart,
but my heart's beat seems to be off. Beat.
See this heart beat is the melody of my weakness,
this heart beat is the tempo of my pain,
this heart beat is the rhythm of my guilt.

When I cry you won't see tears, fall from my eyes,
but you'll hear them cry out from my soul.
As painful as that sounds, it's just a natural cycle.

See when I cry, it's the cleansing of my body.
I'm removing the negativity as I'm longing for
God's arms to be around me.

When I cry, I'm at my weakest,
but God says His grace is sufficient
and His power is made perfect in my weakness.
So even when I'm weak, I am strong
and my heart's beat can find the
right beat

See my heartbeat, is the melody of His strength,
my heartbeat, is the tempo of His grace,
my heartbeat, is the rhythm of His love...
Love...
Love.

So don't be surprised, if when I cry,
you don't see tears
fall
from my eyes.

Part I:

Tainted Eyes

Within the first two years of my graduation from college and receiving my degree in electrical engineering, I spent 16 months unemployed...not how I imagined life after college at all! During my time of unemployment, I tried to stay positive, but doubt slowly crept in. It was hard to keep my head up when every email I opened said, "Thank you for your time, but we have decided to go in a 'different' direction..." What does that even mean!? I took it to mean that I wasn't good enough. I started to question my identity and my self-worth. I started to take residence in a void of negativity with no desire to try anymore. I started to become complacent in my failure and believe I wouldn't do anything substantial with my life. I started to look at my life through ***Tainted Eyes.***

ARMOR

I
wonder if
people can see
through the clothes I
wear, if they know what
is hidden underneath. I wonder if
they are aware that these clothes are
armor, protecting my fragile flesh. Armor
that hides away my insecurities,
armor shielding me from
the daily bullets
of rejection—
shot
from the
guns of life.
Armor that falsely portrays
an image of confidence. What
if they discovered the person they
see, isn't the person underneath?
Would they prefer my
clothes, or would
they prefer,
me?

| | SELF-TAINTED GLASS | |

I stare at my reflection and I don't like what I see. I see an example of what it's like to be an outlaw; and not the rebellious one fighting for a change. I see an outlaw full of disgrace; one whose garments only stay around due to obligation. I gaze in the mirror and I feel its *burden* of having to reflect the image of failure. As my eyes soak in the somber reality, my mind fades to a hopeful fantasy. I imagine a world where my destiny didn't face execution every time I doubted myself. Instead, I access my infinite potential with enough **strength** and **resilience** to make the ~~im~~[possible]. But a mirror only reflects what it sees and there's no changing that. Is there?

THROUGH YOUR EYES

When you look at me, what do you see?

Do you see the cracks in my skin,
or the flaws in my character?
Do you see the holes in my judgement,
or the remnants of my sins?

Do you see my limp when I walk,
can you hear my insecurities when I talk?
Do you notice the hesitation in my breath?
Can you see that when I fight, it's with all I have left?

Can you see my mind, and all the treasures that it holds,
or are you stuck on my smile and all the ugly stories it unfolds?
Are you moved by my actions,
or do you judge me on my image?

Tell me, when you look at me, what do you see?

Do you see a man with confidence,
or do you see a boy plagued with doubts?
Do you see a man striving for success,
or just a boy fighting for acceptance?

Do you see my footprints in the pavement—
have they left a lasting impact?
Do you believe I move with purpose,
or do you think I drag my feet, making my work worthless?

Do you find it hilarious when I fail,
or are you empowered when I get back up?
Do you love me for who I am
or are you blinded by who you think I should be?

When I stand, do you see a man,
slowly unfolding God's plan?

Tell me, what do you see, when you look at me?

DUSK

I no longer operate like myself;
my data has been corrupted—
reformatted without my knowledge.
I've given too many people access to my heart
and they've downloaded unknown software onto
my hard drive. And now, they control me.

I've become a puppet;
lip syncing words from someone else's
mouth. My mind no longer has a creative
thought of its own. My personality is an
unidentified liquid conforming to what
surrounds it. In this case,
the darkness—a void.

I'm living in limbo
and the darkness whispers to me.
The darkness is a verbose poet
lulling me to complacency.

"What if you try and fail?"
"What if you're not meant to
be great?"
"What's the point? Stop trying!"

I believe it.
It's easier to wrap myself in
the warmth of contentment instead
of facing the cold reality of a dream I

feel I can never reach. If I don't try, then
there is no pain, no failure, no
mistakes, no regret. I'll
just sit here in the darkness;
n u m b.

WINDOW PAIN

I look out the window
and I realize that I am a
ship
anchored inside a house—
trapped.

Forced to suppress
the beauty of my
nature.
I never thought I'd be
reduced
to half my worth—
just a sight.

It seems like a
lifetime since
I've sailed, now everyone
questions
my credibility. But a book
still tells a story
no matter how long
it's been
closed.

I'd love to live up to my
purpose,
my potential
but I can't get past this,
window pain.

I'm stuck at a fork
in the road.

I look to my right,
I see the road to happiness;
a life full of purpose and fulfillment.
I can feel the sun soaring high
with a bright yellow and
warm orange mixture.
The sky is the purest shade of
blue
sprinkled with pillow like clouds.
But I also see mountains,
and valleys,
and divots,
and all things that make a journey
long and difficult—
and I'm not strong enough for difficult.
Not anymore.

I look to my left,
I see a path with no ending destination;
an empty life.
The sky is less bright; a faint grey
like the face of sorrow.
The clouds are heavy like the burdens
I carry, and the rain seems endless like the
T.E.A.R.S
from my eyes.
But there's no mountains to climb,
no valleys to overcome,
no divots to avoid.
It's *simple.*

I wouldn't have to live up to anyone's expectations.
I wouldn't have to reach for success and fail.
I could just travel down
a road that's simple and paved,
easy.

I don't know which I prefer…

FREE [DUMB]

My sorrows, my pain,
my times of weakness,
my failures, the same.
Indiscreetly hurt,
noticeably phased,
thoughts of laughter,
comfort me, always.

Opportunity
knocks on the door of
confusion [traps me].
But I see the Light
The key to my *free*—
Dumb [of me to fear].

My sorrow is a choice
My pain is a state.
My weakness has a cure,
My failure is a test

Head down, eyes closed, mind...
free. Infinite prayers keep
me grounded in peace.

BEYOND THE HORIZON

Each season in my life is like chewing gum,
it starts off new, exciting, and flavorful.
But as time passes, the flavor fades
yet, I continue to chew out of habit—
just, going through the motions.

I look out at the horizon,
endless opportunity within reach,
everything the light touches...
but I have no idea what to grasp.

What's the point of having infinite potential
if I can't find what I love?
What fuels my passions?
What gives my life purpose?
What brings honor to my God?

It seems like I've been waiting my entire life,
so now my patience is thin, like *ice*.
Yet, the idea of putting myself out there is
stepping out on ice,
risking it all for...what?

I don't want to be a marker of failure,
an example of what **not** to do.

God, I pray for your discernment—
How do I properly intuit my destiny;
and grasp what is
Beyond, the Horizon...

Part II:

Unplucked Rose Petals

ABOUT TWO MONTHS before I graduated from college, my girlfriend at the time broke up with me. I thought I had processed through those lingering emotions, but as time moved on I found out that I hadn't, and there was a void left in my heart. Our breakup, mixed with my unemployment, made me feel undesirable and alone. I thought to myself, "if I can get somebody to ***want*** *me, then my life would have worth and meaning." So, I started trying to fill this void in my heart with other people. This led me down a dark path where I continuously gave in to my sexual temptations and gave people access to my heart. I learned that lust cannot replace love, and ultimately, just leads to more heartbreak. I was looking for acceptance in people and that caused me to change who I was. I woke up one morning and didn't even recognize my own reflection. I felt dirty, but had no idea how to wash myself clean from my mistakes.*

ADDICTED?

Her presence is *liquor* in my system…

From the moment the sound of her voice
vibrates through my ears
it sends a message to my brain
that **forces** my mouth to smile.
See, before this very moment I felt *empty*,
as if I was missing the very thing I needed to survive…her.

She gets me out of my shell,
she removes my worry,
and she makes me feel…good.
My actions become eccentric,
I forget who I am and
instantly love begins to rain down on my soul;
luckily, I am without an umbrella.
My *soul* desire is to be in her presence
and become high off her beauty;
soft like the purple in the sky.
I am unable to turn away because her smile is **almighty**.

Her touch is a lubricant on my
dry, rough skin
filling the *cracks* left by my insecurities.
Her breathe is like liquid nitrogen—
in small doses it is cool and refreshing.
Her independence leaves me lading on the sideline;
I simply pale in comparison, but I don't mind.

My insides get giddy when she says I'm a bodean*
because no one ever compliments my looks.

Her daily words of affirmation are like clippers to my ego,
keeping it clean, cut, and crisp.
I find myself constantly flushing away people's negative
thoughts like a mental dialysis
because the only words I chose to listen to
are from her personal analysis.

Her presence is *liquor* in my system—
I pray that I don't
get addicted.

* *Bodean: Something or someone that's close to impeccable*

LOVE PURSUIT

I *miss* your love;
so I've been searching for it.
You seem to have misplaced it—
or maybe you threw it away.

I've become an explorer;
sailing over the vast seas of what I thought was your heart,
but it just led to rejection.
I've traveled through the rocky hills of adversity,
eager to become strong enough for you.
And I've climbed to the highest peaks of hope,
trying to reignite the flame of your love—
or at least find it.
I wish I knew its location, so I could retrieve it,
and return it to you.
I'm sorry for making you lose your grip in the first place.

I miss you.
I miss your love.

I *miss* the words we shared,
the moments you made time itself stand still.
Each time you spoke, your words were a waterfall of
genuine care and encouragement.
I *miss* your touch,
gentle yet strong.
I've never experienced a passion as potent as yours;
it must be illegal.
Each time we kissed
your lips injected me with an indescribable love

and our souls intertwined as they
swayed in a synchronized pattern.
I *miss* your love;
so I've been searching for it.
You seem to have misplaced it—
or maybe you threw it away.
It's my fault for making you lose your grip in the first place.

Now I'm going through withdrawals,
taking love tablets, pills,
giving into lust—
searching for the smallest
supplement of your love.

I *miss* the abundance of your love in my life,
so I'm searching for it again.
Is there anything to find?
Or is this the end?

BURIED LOVE

Her eyes reflect my love like a lake reflects the sun.
But when I look deeper I Can see her pain.
Her heart now hidden behind protective walls of apathy,
like a diamond concealed in a safe.

My Love is no longer the combination—
So I try breaking in for her heart,
but she sounds the alarm.
Not sure if I should stay and fight for her love,
or leave and have her hate me.
She seems to have already let go of our love;
so maybe I should release my hold...

But I dream of one day starting a family
and slowly growing old.
I dream of finding a house and making it our home;
filling it with our love,
filling it with our joy,
And making food that speaks to our souls.

I dream of having countless pictures on our wall;
constellations of our memories.
And I dream of having a toy chest,
yes, a toy chest,
to hide away our dearest treasurers—
each other's heart.
But back to Reality...

She took her Exit, so it's time to let her go,
but I'll keep these words buried in my heart,

and hope one day she finds them,
unless our destiny is truly, to always be apart.

ALLURE

When she
entered the room,
her aroma filled the air.

My eyes unwillingly
glanced in her direction,
like metal to a magnet—
mistake number 1.

She had a sleight smile
of confidence, as if she knew
I was caught in her
lustful web.
Her smile reminded me of a
crescent moon
with a soft glow
as if it were stealing
light from another source.

Her essence was
intriguing
and mysterious;
it seemed to follow me.

I failed to turn away
like her gravitational pull was
slowly reeling me in—
we locked eyes,
and she started towards me.

The sway of her hips
stimulated my...

reproductive organs,
I had to turn away—
Who is this woman?
Why is she here, today?
I became timid and stumbled
on my thoughts unable to focus.

She tapped my shoulder
as if knocking on the door
of my existence;
then she spoke to me—
her words, empty.
They were unable to
reach my heart because
it was protected behind my
insulated skin.
But my flesh was
mesmerized
by her eyes,
my thoughts paralyzed.

Her words never
registered in my mind,
I just remember rambling
off 10 numbers I think
were mine.

If I knew then,
what I know now,
I never would have replied
the next day.

HER

When I'm with you I feel nothing.
I've found comfort in an endless void.
I've forgotten how to love;
how to be loved.
I'm afraid of getting back in the game and
learning how to love again.

I thought I *buried* my feelings for *her* in
the bed of the dead
but they've just been in front of me
this whole time.

I realize I'm only with you to get over *her*.
When I think of *her* my roof caves in
and the floor cracks open.
The earth rumbles and everything surrounding me
f a l l s
in.

I think of *her* when I'm with you.
And that's not fair, I know.
But how do I get over someone
I thought was my soul mate?
How do I get over
Her?

CUPID

It hurts to "love" you.
I've been shot by cupid and he's no longer using arrows,
he's using bullets.
You *attempting* to love me
is equivalent to putting a band-aid on my wound;
Simply.
Not.
Enough.

Instead of healing
you are making things worse; infection.
From the moment we kissed we poisoned
our relationship.
We opened a door we never
should have had the key to unlock and
now we are forced to walk in the
mess
we
created.

It's times like this I wish I could
sleep away my mistakes;
craft them into a single nightmare
and then just...wake up.
Forget the
whole
thing
happened.

It's times like this I wish
I could bottle my emotions,
throw them over board and then
fly on the wings of my
freedom
and soar high
above the mountains life placed
in my path.
It's times like this I wish that we never locked eyes
because from that moment
I became trapped in your gaze;
willing to do anything
you asked. And
I
hate
that.

See,
it hurts to "love" you.
You *attempting* to love me
is equivalent to putting a band-aid on my wound;
Simply.
Not.
Enough.

DRIP

You are warm water, falling on my skin,
defrosting the parts of my body abandoned by *love.*
But after you drip through my pain;
which makes up my 5'10 figure, you leave.
And I'm left loveless. Abandoned. Broken.

You are the answer to the wrong question,
only adding to the problem, not the solution.
No matter how warm you feel on my skin,
no matter how much of my body you defrost with *your, "love"*
When you leave, I'm still wet,
with no one to protect my heart.
Broken—
with no one to build me back up.
Abandoned—
with no one to guide me, *home.*

You are warm water, falling on my skin,
defrosting the parts of my body abandoned by *love.*
Just a temporary fix, as you drip through my heart,
and abandon, **my love.**

CASTMATES

The spotlight is on us,
this is just a performance
and we are improvising—
mimicking what we see on TV;
acting like we are in love.

Even still,
your presence is captivating,
your mind is infatuating,
your body is…sexy.

At night,
I am unable to sleep
because my flesh is craving to be with you;
to know you intimately and fully, damn.

I try to think of something else
but all I hear is your laugh
and I smile;
and you stay on my mind.

But I don't want to think about you.
I don't want to be in the spotlight anymore
because this is just a performance,
and I am tired of improvising—
acting like we are in love.

EXIT 67

How do I wash myself clean from this…dirt?

I try lathering my heart in the love from my heavenly father
but the receipts of your betrayal linger in my veins
and become poison, paralyzing my limbs.

I sit in this seat motionless
reminiscing on our time together.
I thought you were my vacation
but really you were my jail cell.

I was unlawfully arrested for my debt—
Foolish of me to take out a loan from your bank
but I thought I was in desperate need of the money,
I mean love.

And just as I began to trust you, you vanished
to some remote location
like the sun does at night
but you never shined as bright
you just absorbed my light…
and now I'm abandoned.

If love is a highway
then I am stranded on the side
of the road off exit 67
with nothing left in my tank…

Trying to wash myself clean from this…dirt.

VISIONARY

I turned around and was shocked by what I saw,
Something so magnificent, words can't describe,
Yet I'll try.

There she was, 5 foot 6.
Bundled up from head to toe,
Looking off into the distance as if she has nowhere to go.
She was mesmerized by the city line and
I was mesmerized by her presence.
Brown boots and blue jeans,
Purple coat and grey scarf.
I walked closer to ensure I wasn't being deceived.

I began to speak, but words left me.
I tried to lift my hand and wave, but it became too heavy.
We made eye contact and I began to melt.
Her eyes as bright as the sun yet as gentle as the moon.
Softly caressing my heart as it beats to her tune.
We became an orchestra playing in unison.
Our eyes played the melody
As our blinks harmonized with our breathing
And our hearts kept the beat.

She smiled, and her love was felt.
My strength was renewed and my unknown pain was removed
But then she walked away, into the distance.

I turned around and was shocked by what I saw,
Brown blobs with white squares,
Silver crosses and medical tools.
I was in the emergency room and
I realized I had seen my guardian angel.

Part III:

Letters to Heaven

Mentally I was questioning the significance of my life, emotionally I was recovering from my heartbreak, physically I was battling my lust, and spiritually; I was a mess. I started to distance myself from God, blaming him for all my hardships. I found it hard to believe that He loved me if He allowed me to go through such negativity and feel so horrible about myself. I started to bottle my emotions because it was too painful to address them. I just wanted to forget my past, but I knew I couldn't just ignore it forever. Almost a year passed before I got tired of accepting defeat and I wrote these ***Letters to Heaven.***

MEMOIR

I remember when I used to pray
and feel your love on a molecular level.
With each word I shared you took a
visit into the depths of my soul,
you explored the city of my mind—
which you created.

You established my foundation and built the
pillars of my faith.
You paved a path for my purpose—
in some seasons a trail,
in others a highway. Regardless,
you always made it so I'd reach my destination.
You watched me as I grew,
from your window you had the best view…

I remember when the enemy
snuck in the back door and trapped
me in a state of dubiety.
Putting road blocks on my path,
abolishing my pillars,
and creating permanent cracks in my foundation.

I stopped praying.
I stopped trying.
I stopped trusting.

You became the
sole
reason for all my problems.
All the pain that I was experiencing;

the rejection I was facing,
was due to your lack of power,
and lack of *love.*

I never hated you.
I just questioned your timing,
your power,
my purpose,
and your *plan.*
My faith dwindled becoming
a thing of the past,
a forgotten
memory...

NIGHTLIGHT

I've lost my trust in you—
the light of your *promise* is no
longer illuminating the
darkness of my doubt.

What *purpose* could you
possibly have...
for *me?*

[ ]

My circumstance makes me believe that a
touch
from you is a burden;
a leash—
preventing me from straying,
preventing me from living.
I feel like if I'm living with you then I'm not
[free]

[IN]FLECTION

My body is motionless as I stand in a stupor watching a dog with midnight fur hide his bone in the ground. I mentally dig myself into a deeper and deeper hole, slowly getting further and further away from you.

Stupidity—
the only explanation for making the same mistake over and over. I should have paid more attention to your warning. You told me my happiness was my decision and my heartbreaks weren't accidents if I continuously drove into *love collisions* with no regard for my heart. No protection. Now my heart is numb, no song can give it a beat, no music can depict its sorrow, no painting can illustrate its pain.

I allowed my insecurities to flood my faith, I allowed her words to dance over my heart, I allowed sin to come in and flip my life upside down, and I allowed the enemy to trap me.

Question is, am I too far gone?

I've stepped out of your light, living in the shadow of my potential, constantly faced with failure after failure. Unfamiliar whispers echo through my ears discouraging any further efforts. I walk in misery, I drag my feet through its pain, I sit in its negativity.

God. Help. Me.

BULLETPROOF

Life has made me **bulletproof.**
Adversity has required me to take up
self-made *armor*
in attempt to protect myself.
My heartbreak refuses to let anyone in—
not even you.

I've been hurt in the past
and I refuse to be hurt again.
I've thickened my skin and
hardened my heart—
I'm **bulletproof.**
So why am I still hurting?

This *armor* that I wear,
this **bulletproof** skin I put on
doesn't protect me from the pain,
but just keeps it concealed.
I am forced to carry it around like a
burden.

I don't have the strength
to remove the bondage around
my scars. I'm afraid to
surrender
my life to you and be healed
because it isn't easy to let go of
what I've been clinging to.

But you—
You are a different kind of bullet;

a celestial force
with the ability to pierce through my pride,
removing the infection
of my ego and
healing the wounds inflicted
by my choices,
by my mistakes.

I want to be free from this
burden,
these chains.
I want to be healed.

Help me take off this *armor,*
I don't want to be bulletproof
anymore.

MY PRAYER

Dear Lord,

I come to you today, not sure what to ask or even say. I just know that I need to be here, and I need to pray. Pray for guidance and pray for your help—pray for my friends and pray for myself. Lord, I pray for courage and endurance and I pray that you bless me with the ability of perseverance. I pray that you turn my negatives into positives and help me through these situations that make me feel like you're not fulfilling your promises. Because to be completely honest, I can't count how many times I've broken my promise. So, Lord, I pray for a change and that you start to heal because I feel the enemy starting to **kill** my soul and **kill** my spirit. This is some sad news, but I have to say it, they have to hear it, and I have to trust in you to fix it!

God, I've been running back to you for the longest time. It's taken so long because I always get distracted and follow the wrong signs. So, I pray for clarity, that you show me the right path and I stick to it. I pray for obedience, that I stop asking questions and just do it. And I pray for security, that I can accept who you have created me to be. That I can find myself and declare who I am—without fear, without doubt, and without lies coming from my mouth; without regret, without guilt, and without being covered with the enemy's filth.

God my wounds go deeper, but my words don't properly show how I feel, so listen to my heart and let my desires be revealed. Lord my heart's crying out:

Help me through the heartache, and through all the pain. Through all my worries, help me walk through the rain. Help me through all my doubts and all my shame. Through all my struggles and through the enemy's games. Help me through tribulations, and all my trials. Through temptations that last for a while. Show me your strength, fill me with faith, and give me your love, all I can take. Show me your glory, fill me with hope, help me to stand, and help me to cope. Because Lord I want to turn away from sin, I want to be able to fully walk with you again, ***but,*** *I know I've made many mistakes, so I pray that you take them away.*

Lord, I know that you care, so please, please answer my prayer.

Amen.

MY SON,

Where are you?

Please come home, you've be gone for too long. I know that you're hurting, that you're questioning yourself and these series of events. Let me help you.

Although you've been *gone,* I've never left your side. This distance between us was a figment of your imagination. I was always there pleading for you to walk on the path I paved for you.

I wept as you turned away and I wept as you cried. I wept at your choices and the pain they created. I wept as you set motionless in the dark, ignorant of your purpose. I wept for you.

I wept as I witnessed the joy fade from your smile, the passion dissipate from your eyes, and the purpose vanish from your touch.

But listen—
I have a plan for you. The things you asked for, endurance, clarity, strength, and love; couldn't just be handed to you, but required a journey. I couldn't give you endurance without first giving you something to endure. The clarity you seeked, required your eyes to be open to who I am and who I created you to be. While I am the same, you are forever growing and changing. To receive strength, you had to overcome obstacles and pain. And to know love, you had to first know me. I am love and you will never know a love greater than me.

I have forgiven you of all your sins so don't mistake the darkness as a punishment. For a light serves no purpose in a room that is already lit, but a light has purpose in illuminating the darkness. See, I have a plan for you.

I understand your decisiveness in trusting me because you have been mistreated in the past, but I am not like man. My touch is not a leash, *My yoke is easy, My burden is light.* Stop giving your heart to people of the world because they can't help you, but I can, and I will mend your brokenness.

Stop trying to be successful on your own, let me help you. Please just come home.

My son, *where are you?*

IN REALITY

In reality,
I was going through misery…
I'm letting it all out, so you can
feel me.
Everyday aiming for perfection,
but
getting
knocked
down by
R E J E C T I O N.

I wanted to get smarter,
I wanted to get stronger,
I wanted to get faster,
I wanted to get better,
but instead I'm reciting this letter—

This letter I wrote to God
praying for his protection to
rain
over me because
I was lost with no D
I
R
E
C
T
I
O
N

I allowed doubts to fill my mind,
leaving my faith far behind.
I was filled with hesitation,
and felt trapped by my
T.E.A.R.S
of desperation.
I longed to feel the Lord's love
and its marvelous sensation;
so I could find my destination,
and touch people all across this
nation—
But I was caught in mid

R
O
T N
A O
T I

I turned my back on the Lord,
so my life was no longer on one accord.
I allowed the enemy
to come within me
and fill my life with pain,
now are you feelin' me?

He came into my life to
steal,
kill,
and destroy—
Leaving my love for the Lord virtually
nulled and void.

He tried *stealing* my faith
to separate me from my father,
so I would no longer try or even bother.
He tried *killing* my hope,
so when temptation came, I couldn't cope.
And he tried *destroying* my desire to go around tellin' people
that one day we'd be reunited in heaven.

I became confused and weak,
looked all around but didn't know what to
~~seek.~~
I felt the *corruption* in my heart,
and saw my life
F
A
L
L
I
N
G
a p a r t.
I no longer felt comfortable around my friends,
and I prayed for the day for it to finally
e n d.

But I had to pret*end*
to fit in,
with people whose lives were filled with sin;
and I felt like a failure again
and again;
and asked the Lord,
"When, when will I win!?"

I started listening to negative voices,
and in return made some horrible choices—
I knew what was right,
but blinded my sight,
by lowering my
defenses,
almost losing the fight.

But just as I felt I could go no more,
a power came over me like never before.
It was the Lord showing his love and grace,
which took me out of that dark cruel place,
allowing me to finish my
r a c e.

I always thought I was running alone,
but the Lord was always beside me,
so I was never on my own.
He put me through all those trials and tribulations,
because that's how he helps his creations
to o v e r c o m e
t e m p t a t i o n s.

Nothing,
was ever too hard for me to handle,
not even the enemy trying to vandal-ize,
all my tries,
to see past his lies,
by opening my eyes,
to the prize
of the Lord's glory
and to realize;
that ***I can do all things through Christ who strengthens me.***

I just have to see myself
r e a c h i n g
victory,
and believe
that I can achieve
all things I set my mind to,
so now I guarantee;
that it won't always be easy,
but it **will**
always
be worth it.
So I'm embracing the God in me
because I choose to
w o r s h i p.

Part IV:

The Sentries

A SENTRY IS A WARRIOR charged with the task of protecting a gate or entrance. In our life, we have people we consider to be a sentry; people that we trust to protect, fight, and defend us. They help carry our burdens, and we see them as invincible. We don't always see the things that challenge them or the things they have struggled through. We don't take the time to look behind their smile. But, a sentry, no matter how strong, has situations they wish they would have handled differently and moments when they need help.

MERCURY

I'm convinced that I'm destined to be
alone;
orbiting around my failures—
caught in their gravitational pull.

My brothers—
my support system
light years away, unable to help
me.

I move quickly past discouragement
but find myself in its company just
the same.
I can't escape this cycle—
this never-ending journey
to find happiness.
To find love,
or just…a friend.

I feel inadequate,
unable to provide for those that depend on
me
because I am too close to the
heat of my past.
I need help.
I need
        to break free.

ROOFTOP SYMPHONY

Inhale

My mind races as I watch
f i r e
dance over a dried flower mixture
turning it into a gas
that penetrates my lungs
and begins stimulating my brain cells...

Exhale

My thoughts become smoke
floating above my head and
form humanoid figures
moving to a distant melody...
life.

They move with a
contained freedom.
Some are dancing,
others are singing,
But the ones I find most intriguing
have instruments.
Instruments hand crafted to fit
between the cracks of their fingers
and produce a unique sound that
only the breath between their lips
can create.

I envy them.
They live a life full of

passion and purpose.
No conductor.

Inhale

See,
success is my conductor;
I am just another musician in the orchestra
following his instruction.
I try staying on his beat,
but my heart as one of its own.
I try following his rhythm,
but my life has a path of its own.

Exhale

My goals become smoke
floating above my head and
form a humanoid figure
playing a heart-rending melody…

It's me, I've found my instrument;
the one life welded for me
to play and complete the
unsung song of my purpose.

I play with a balance of
freedom, happiness, and success.
My sound impacts those around me
and they are empowered
to reach their goals.
I am no longer forced to play at the
instruction
of another. I am my own success.

I am my own

conductor.

CALYPSO

Before
I heard your **obnoxious** laugh from across the room,
my heart was like the sea—
free, and unobtainable.
But as I got up to leave
I mistakenly glanced in your direction and
saw the radiating glow of your
golden honey skin;
and at that moment I saw into the
depths of your mind.
Damn.

I
casually strolled into your presence
where we began to
d a n c e
with our words.
I marveled at our similarities and
the way you stared at me with those
dark, green eyes
a n d
crooked smile,
suggested you felt the
same.

Time
escaped me; I blinked, we were transported to your
apartment, ripping clothes off until our skin was bare.
I loved kissing on your
full, juicy lips;

and feeling your *hips*—on my body.
Your *hips* moved to the beat of the ocean
creating waves that enveloped my skin with…
pleasure.
Then you rocked us both into a peaceful
slumber.

Days
passed and you became a permanent resident
of my mind. My fingers grew
a n x i o u s
unless they were texting you. I enjoyed cuddling,
resting in your presence—discovering the
constellations of your beauty,
hidden in your *freckles.*
We developed an
undying love—
parading around the phrase, "I love you"
like a game of
Taboo.

Until
the day came when you had to leave. We
knew our love was
t e m p o r a r y;
for we were characters from
two different stories. We began to speak like
s t r a n g e r s
with a subtext of lovers as I painfully watched you drift away from me.
You looked at me with your now
soft, green eyes
as if you saw into the depths of my
mind.

I
took one final
g l a n c e
and felt the radiating glow of your
golden, honey skin;
and wish I had said,
"I love you."
Damn.

KING OF THE JUNGLE

He is *burdened* by responsibility
and strengthened by
l o v e
His ancestors taught him to strive for greatness
and give thanks to the Lord
a b o v e

He always learns from his mistakes
and puts his best foot
f o r w a r d
He protects those in his circle—
he's a walking shield; around him they see no
h o r r o r

He isn't the smartest, the strongest,
the fastest, or the
b e s t
But he is versatile, always progressing,
demolishing negativity, and prowling on
s u c c e s s

He is patient, and trusting,
and fierce, and
h u m b l e
He does not brag in his success, but
shows confidence in his work
He is
K i n g O f T h e J u n g l e

FORTRESS OF ILLUSION(S)

He replied, "Because you have so little faith. Truly I tell you, if you have faith as small as a mustard seed, you can say to this mountain, 'Move from here to there,' and it will move. Nothing will be impossible for you.
Matthew 17:20

A million drops of water fall on my skin and remind me of the tears that I've cried; like when she nearly died. I was eleven; physically weak, petrified. She laid on the couch in silence as if it were her deathbed, but I could hear the screams of her pain calling out from the pits of her soul. I sat on the steps crying, trying to be strong. Each teardrop was a prayer and the outpour of my eyes flooded my face creating vast oceans of faith that filled the wells of my heart.

"Help Her...God!"

I became the eye of a spiritual hurricane; breaking down the levies of doubt, flooding the shores of her pain and blowing away all fears creating a clear path for God to heal. My faith didn't allow any room for her not be okay. I prayed for her strength, her resilience, and her health.

I was fierce, what changed?

Now—
I stand in the shower and a million drops of water fall on my skin and remind me of all the tears that I've cried; the moments I felt so weak that I could die. I'm twenty-five; physically at my prime yet spiritually... it's like I hit rewind. I try to solve life's problems on my own. No prayers. No help.

"I can do this on my own."

But I've become the victim of life's emotional hurricane; the levies of my faith broken down by treacherous winds of doubt, my shores of peace flooded with pain, and my mind destroyed by reality. I try punching my way through debris, I try thinking my way out to be free; but the storm is never ending. I'm left stranded, full of fear with no strength left.

"I think...I think I need help, God"

A million drops of water fall on my skin and remind me of all the tears that I've cried; the times I told myself I was strong enough to handle life on my own; but clearly, I lied.

TIME CAPSULE

Only time knows my
secret,
not that I am ashamed of my past,
but no one cared enough to ask.
I remember

the days I had to force myself
out of bed,
out of the house.
I remember

being embarrassed that I had
to use food stamps to buy groceries
and apply for a monthly unemployment check.
I remember

having the front row seat to the movie
of my life,
disappointed
with the main character's inability to
overcome this strife. I found myself
wanting to yell,
"cut!"
as if I were the director.
I remember

My struggle.
My failure.
My mistakes.

But God
created this beauty called time,

and she's been keeping my

secret.

Over these past two years
I've been blessed
and I've been growing.
I am not the man I used to be,
and thank God they don't see that man,
they just see me.
They didn't see my come up
or understand my progress,
but they recognized my grit because
I refused to let my circumstance
define me,
but my circumstance helped me
find me.

How could I appreciate my high
if I never experienced a low?
How could I expect the seeds of my potential to sprout,
if I never took time to sow?
Now I'm reaping blessings—
fruit I forgot I planted,
happily walking in my new season.

I don't need time to keep my

secret

anymore, because I want you to be a witness.

MEET THE AUTHOR

Sleight was born Robert E. Timmons II in December of 1992 to the parents of Robert and Arnetta Timmons. He is the middle child of three, born and raised in Houston, Texas. Robert didn't find his love of poetry until his senior year of high school when he found spoken word poetry as an artistic way to express himself through stressful times. Upon graduating from high school in 2011, Robert attended the University of Pittsburgh and pursued a degree in electrical engineering. He always had a skill, understanding, and love for mathematics and engineering seemed like a very logical way to utilize his skillset. Throughout college, Robert was very involved around campus as he continued to develop his artistic expression. He continued to write and perform spoken word poetry all over campus and the city of Pittsburgh. Robert even had the opportunity to be casted as one of the lead characters, Eugene, in the University of Pittsburgh Theatre Department's adaptation of *Yellowman* by Dael Orlandersmith. Since then, Robert has continued to hone in on his artistic talent and plans to continue writing, performing, and acting. This book is only the beginning...

Made in the USA
Middletown, DE
27 July 2018